D1525818

I take great pleasure in applauding the advent of the Ubu Repertory Theater Publications. Devoted to bringing English versions of important contemporary dramatic works from French-speaking countries, this program could not be more important or timely when institutions such as the Eugene O'Neill Theater Center and the Milwaukee Repertory Theater have begun to embrace and espouse the cause of this key element of cultural exchange.

It is particularly important to realize that the plays chosen for translation and publication are not part of any specific genre, but rather are eclectic and are selected to inform the English-speaking public of the scope and richness of present-day French-speaking playwrights.

I cherish the hope that this marvelous project will spark a renaissance in professional collaboration between our French and English-speaking theaters and foster greater understanding between diverse national groups.

George C. White, President
Eugene O'Neill Memorial Theater Center

625177

UBU REPERTORY THEATER PUBLICATIONS

1. Yves Navarre, *Swimming Pools at War*.

2. Bernard-Marie Koltès, *Night Just Before the Forest* and *Struggle of the Dogs and the Black*.

3. Michel Tournier, *The Fetishist*.

4. Jean-Paul Aron, *The Office*.

5. Jean-Paul Wenzel, *Far From Hagondange* and *Vater Land, the Country of our Fathers*.

6. Madeleine Laïk, *Deck Chairs*.

7. Pierre Bourgeade, *The Passport* and *The Door*.

8. Andrée Chedid, *The Showman*.

9. Jean-Luc Lagarce, *Madame Knipper's Journey to Eastern Prussia*.

10. Denise Bonal, *Family Portrait*.

11. Daniel Besnehard, *Passengers*.

12. Enzo Cormann, *Cabale*.

13. Protais Asseng, *Enough is Enough*.

14. Aimé Césaire, *A Tempest*.

15. Bernard Dadié, *Monsieur Thôgô-gnini*.

16. Tchicaya u Tam'Si, *The Glorious Destiny of Marshal Nnikon Nniku*.

17. Sony Lab'ou Tansi, *Parentheses of Blood*.

This publication is made possible, in part, with public funds from the New York State Council on the Arts.

BERNARD B. DADIÉ

MONSIEUR THÔGÔ-GNINI

Translated from the French

by **Townsend Brewster**

Ubu Repertory Theater Publications

Printed in the United States of America
1986

ISSN 0738-4009
ISBN 0-913745—16-2

MONSIEUR THÔGÔ-GNINI

CHARACTERS

THÔGÔ-GNINI
N'ZEKOU
YA-GBA
BOUADI
FAKRON
BROUBA
AKABOUA
THE JUDGE
THE COURT CLERK
THE USHER
A POLICEMAN
A NEWSBOY
A WAITER
A BEGGAR
A BOY
A SERVANT
A STRANGE BEING
AN AFRICAN KING
A GRINNING OLD MAN
A WEEPING WOMAN
A SMILING CHILD

A HERALD
A CAFE SINGER
A WHITE MESSENGER
A TRADER
A MAN OF THE CROWD
ELDER WHITE MAN
YOUNGER WHITE MAN
THREE TOUGHS
AN ACOLYTE
A COOPER
TWO NATIVE PORTERS
A GOLD-DUST BEARER
REPRESENTATIVES OF:
  GOOD FAITH
  GRATITUDE
  SENECTITUDE
  TRADITION
  WOMAN
  CHILD
  LOVE
  DRAMA
TWO YOUNG MEN (N'ZEKOU'S SONS)
A WOMAN IN THÔGÔ-GNINI'S HOUSE
CROWD, SERVANTS, POLICEMAN,
  VENDORS, TRADERS

FIRST TABLEAU

THE VILLAGE

(At Curtain, an African King, in the midst of a rather unruly Crowd who are singing and dancing, is on stage. He is borne in a hammock. Softly, we hear "Old Man River." The year is 1840 when many "been-tos" have returned to this country on the coast of West Africa. Enter a White Trader and an Acolyte followed by two Native Porters. After their arrival, the singing and dancing cease. Thôgô-gnini, the King's cane-bearer, is present dressed in the native costume.)

TRADER *(with mock reverence)* All hail to thee, great King, on whose empire the sun never sets.

THÔGÔ-GNINI The sun never sets on the truth. What night conceals, daylight reveals. What brings you to this country, White man?

TRADER God has directed my steps to you, to the Black sun, your king. I've been two months at sea and survived countless storms.

THÔGÔ-GNINI Welcome. The king and the people wish you happiness in this land.

TRADER The king and his people?

1

THÔGÔ-GNINI   No. The king and the people.

TRADER   Your king's reputation for power has spread as far as the shores of my native land. Wind-borne, it fills the sails of every ship. Therefore, in passing, I'm here to present the cordial greetings of my own king.

THÔGÔ-GNINI   Of course, the wind, the birds, the waves sing of the greatness of our king. He holds in his august hands the lives of the tribes of this nation. Clearly, God has guided you to us.

TRADER   Yes. I've passed through a thousand dangers to bring you the greetings of my king. But then, what herald bearing an interregal message would not have braved every obstacle?

THÔGÔ-GNINI   Who can handcuff an elephant? Who can eclipse the *éclat* of the sun? Who can pick up a raindrop? The thunder has filled the heavens with its voice to make you aware that our great king is the only great king on Earth, the king of kings.

TRADER   Yes, we've heard as much through our seamen, our tradesmen, our traders. We take particular note of anything going on within your borders. These people of the sun are especially dear to us; they're at the heart of all our dreams.

THÔGÔ-GNINI   The sun! Ah, the sun! The sun!

2

TRADER   If you knew the rigors of northern climates, you'd appreciate the sun even more, not to mention your eternally verdurous vistas filled with the songs of birds and the hum of insects.

THÔGÔ-GNINI   The sun! The sun! Here's what the sun does. *(He points to his black skin.)*

TRADER   Never mind about that. The sun! The light! Those trees jutting toward the stars as if to transmit the ardor of your prayers to them, the substance of your songs, the rhythm of your dances! Tom-tom! Tom-tom! Tom-tom!

(Tom-toms beat. Dance.)

THÔGÔ-GNINI   Stranger from across the sea, the pillar of humanity, in other words, our great king, he who, with a wave of his hand, can annihilate hundreds and hundreds of nations, this master of the rain and the sun, he into whose presence misfortune never sets foot, he who intimidates and each day defies death . . . this great king has commanded a dance in your honor. As of now, you're one of us.

TRADER   Let me express my gratitude to His Majesty. May Heaven prolong his days on this Earth!

(Dance.)

And there's more. I've not come empty-handed. I've

been instructed to deliver this robe to your king.

(Organ music. The Trader, having signaled for the Royal Attendants to remove the King's jewels, gives him the robe. Tom-toms join their beat to the organ music. The Trader produces a wig.)

A wig for the protection of royal heads. As much as the father of any other nation, the father of your nation needs one. A good wig, be it blond, brown, or auburn, whatever, but the important thing is for a crowned head to sport a wig. And, finally, we come to this crown and this sceptre.

(The Crowd sings and dances joyously.)

It's now my duty to inform you that the exit of a king as mighty as yours, must follow the rules. The crowd must line up on both sides of the street to applaud, wave little flags, and flourish palm branches. *(He arranges the Crowd in double file.)* A king towers over the people. Never forget that. He is of a different essence, a different blood. Black or not, he has blue blood, and, before his blue blood, everyone must bow down, beginning with those whose blood is a mere red.

(The King gets up, takes a few steps, goes back, and sits down.)

THÔGÔ-GNINI The king is greatly pleased with everything his colleague, your king, has sent him. In return, he requests you to take to him a few jars of gold dust and the gold-dust bearer.

TRADER   This little boy?

THÔGÔ-GNINI   Yes.

TRADER   For me or for the king?

THÔGÔ-GNINI   He's a portion of the king's gift.

TRADER   (aside) Strange gifts.

THÔGÔ-GNINI   I beg your pardon?

TRADER   My king has imposed another duty on me, that of setting up trade negotiations between our kingdoms. We need palm oil. My king would be happy to make you his sole supplier.

THÔGÔ-GNINI   Palm oil? Palm oil!

TRADER   A new form of slave-trade replacing the old.

(The Men pass rifles among one another.)

I'll grant you these rifles are antiquated, but they'll still do the job.

THÔGÔ-GNINI   The king would like to know whether their purpose is to put an end to war.

TRADER   *(with authority)* Naturally. To silence rifles the whole world over.

   (A gun goes off.)

THÔGÔ-GNINI   The king would like to know why you manufacture so many rifles.

TRADER   In order to eliminate war. To annihilate war.

   (The Crowd bursts out laughing.)

CROWD   To annihilate war by manufacturing rifles and selling rifles! Ha! Ha! Ha! Ha!

   (A second gun goes off.)

THÔGÔ-GNINI   The great king says he understands perfectly and so do the people, but asks who, if there were no more war, would work the palm groves.

TRADER   Why, the men you've already rounded up.

THÔGÔ-GNINI   Where should we keep them?

TRADER   We'll teach you to build prisons to pen them up in. These men will compose your reservoir of free labor.

THÔGÔ-GNINI   How long may we keep them?

TRADER   What a question! Two years, twenty years, fifty years. Judge each case on its merits according to the rank and station of the prisoner, according to your daily whim, according to the condition of your stomach, your liver.

THÔGÔ-GNINI   The king understands but would like to know how many prisons there are in your country.

TRADER   Each city boasts at least two prisons; since the kingdom contains a minimum of nine hundred cities, that makes about . . . one thousand eight hundred prisons.

CROWD   (*muttering*) Hmmm. Hmm.

A MAN   Will there be any free men left?

TRADER   Certainly, certainly. There'll be thousands to walk around doing as they please.

THÔGÔ-GNINI   Won't they be merely on probation?

TRADER   No, no. You don't understand. We're the most humane people in the world. Our land is where liberty luxuriates. A liberty tree stands in every city. No country has more liberty trees than ours.

(*The Crowd breaks ranks.*)

No, no, stay in line, in long lines. That's order; that's

discipline, the might of armies, of nations: One God, one king, and subjects.

THÔGÔ-GNINI   The king understands. We've reached the heart of the vast space our king occupies in your king's esteem.

TRADER   I know you believe in God, in spirits, in ghosts; I know you consult oracles; in a word, you believe in God, but God is far away.

CROWD   Oh, far, indeed, far, indeed . . . . Way up in the sky, far away, extremely far away.

TRADER   Up in the sky? Hmmm. I couldn't say. Even my king, whose right to the throne is divine, couldn't say. What I can say is we're here on Earth and that, on Earth, we must live with a visible god, a tangible god. (*He takes bundles of bank notes from his pockets.*) Such as this.

CROWD   Money!

THÔGÔ-GNINI   Money! Money! Give it here!

TRADER   No, you'll have to earn it by the sweat of your brow. You'll have to plant lots of palm trees, lots of peanuts. Europe needs them. So get rich quick.

THÔGÔ-GNINI   Money! Money!

TRADER With money, you build a country, you main-
tain a country. We Whites have a bad reputation, but
the other races follow our example. Remember that, in
our country, a woman's pet name for her man is my
little cabbage, my little bunny, my little duck; corres-
pondingly, her man calls happy times "palmy days;"
that means women raise cabbages and ducks; whereas
men raise palm trees. *(He displays two bundles of bank
notes.)* You must work . . . work!

CROWD *(with enthusiasm)* Money! Money!

THÔGÔ-GNINI Our great king, your good king's
cousin, approves of your proclamation. Here, he is the
refulgent sun as, back where you come from, your king
is the one and only moon. They were created to understand each other and rule the world. Tell your mighty
king he's become the White king of the Blacks and our
king is now the Black king of the Whites. May this little
boy with whom he presents you, serve to cement this
friendship that he wishes to gleam more resplendently
than the sun of your skies and the sun of our skies put
together, to run deeper than your sea and our sea
combined, to be truer than your truth and our truth in
tandem.

*(Song. The King stands and gets back into his hammock.
Exeunt.)*

CURTAIN.

9

SECOND TABLEAU

THE PALM GROVE

(A palm grove. For a while, the beat of tom-toms drowns out "Old Man River" in evidence of the gradual change of conditions. Work songs alternate with the tom-toms and "Old Man River" as if each, in turn, were borne on the wind, but, as the tom-toms and the work songs predominate, "Old Man River" becomes a muted undercurrent like an echo from the other side of the Atlantic. On one side of the stage, are barrels of oil and bunches of palm branches carried by Women. Men roll kegs of palm oil. Black Messengers and White Traders bustle to and fro. A Cooper is repairing barrels. Women and Children are pounding palm seeds. From the rear of the auditorium, Monsieur Thôgô-gnini watches the proceedings. He is dressed Western-style in a Panama hat, trousers, walking stick; he is smoking a big cigar, and he has acquired a "corporation." Enter a White Messenger.)

WHITE MESSENGER   Speed it up! Speed it up! I'm in a terrible rush! Bloody hell! You're forgetting time is money. Can you still be thinking of dawdling? Now hear this! Now hear this! You will get wise. Speed it up!

(Enter Monsieur Thôgô-gnini.)

THÔGÔ-GNINI   Are you treating us as a conquered people?

10

WHITE MESSENGER   As of now, plant palm trees, coconuts, peanuts. Everything else will follow in due course. Speed it up! Speed it up!

THÔGÔ-GNINI   Oh?

WHITE MESSENGER   *(to Thôgô-gnini)* You'll be our most valued assistant.

THÔGÔ-GNINI   Oh? *(To the Workers)* Speed it up!

WHITE MESSENGER   And you'll acquire innumerable honors by virtue of getting rich, filthy rich. We'll enrich you.

THÔGÔ-GNINI   *(to himself as he starts off)* Money! Money! Innumerable honors! *(To the Workers.)* Speed it up!

(The tom-tom beat increases in intensity, and the singing swells until it fills the auditorium.)

WHITE MESSENGER   Speed it up! Speed it up! I'm pressed for time, and time is money. Speed it up! Speed it up!

(The Workers increase the speed of their efforts to an hysterical pace.)

THÔGÔ-GNINI   (*to himself*) Money! Innumerable
honors! Money! (*To the Workers.*) Speed it up! Speed it
up!

CURTAIN

THIRD TABLEAU

THE DREAM

(Enter a Strange Being, half White, half Black, and clad in the skins of the lion, the panther, the hyena, and adorned with the feathers of the peacock, the eagle, the crow, in his belt, a revolver, and, in his hand, a rifle in a bandolier. Monsieur Thôgô-gnini is discovered asleep.)

BEING   Who can pin me down? I'm White; I'm Black; I'm lion, leopard, panther, hyena, crow, eagle; I'm everything; I'm nothing. I'm the past; I'm the future. I'm . . . what I am. If I weren't what I am, then I shouldn't be . . . what I am. When I live well, everybody lives well as does the state. When I'm in good health, you're all in good health as is the state. I'm every color. All things mix and combine in me. I'm all others; all others are I. The city is I, and I am the city. I'm the present; I need to live; I'm the future; it's my duty to be alive today.

(Highly distinguished Men and Women cross the stage, their hands extended.)

You may pass through, Your Worships, as soon, Excellencies, as you've paid. It's the toll. Pay, pay. I've seized the city. Pay, Your Worships. I'm lion, panther, leopard, eagle, crow. Pay! Who are you?

GOOD FAITH   Good Faith.

BEING   Good Faith! Don't know ya. *(He shoots him.)* And you?

GRATITUDE   Gratitude.

BEING   Gratitude! Don't know ya. *(He shoots him.)* And you?

SENECTITUDE   Senectitude. Respect for age.

BEING   Respect for age? For what age? Respect in what respect? And why? Respect for age, don't know ya. *(He shoots him.)* And you?

TRADITION   Tradition.

BEING   Hmmm. So you're Tradition. That dead weight, Tradition, that ball and chain on the feet of generations. Gangway! Give me space! *Lebensraum!* Tradition, don't know ya. *(He shoots him.)* And you?

WOMAN   Woman.

BEING   Woman! No! You've forfeited your place among men. Smiles, caresses, compassion. No, you're sadly out of date. Woman, don't know ya. *(He shoots her.)* And you?

CHILD   I?

BEING   You? Of course, you.

CHILD   Child.

BEING   Child?

CHILD   Yes, Child.

BEING   In other words?

CHILD   The future.

BEING   The future! Oh! Oh! Oh! The future! I'm the future. I'm the present. Future, don't know ya. *(He shoots him.)* Who objects? Who even considers objecting? Move on, Your Worships. Move on, Excellencies. Pay, Excellencies. You're also the future, also the present. It's you who keep me going. Pay, Your Worships. Pay, Excellencies. And you?

LOVE   Love.

BEING   Love! Love! Now, you're the one I've been waiting for. You! You who've been disrupting the world since who knows when. Love for whom? Love for what? Hollow word! Old worn out word! No, money, power, tributes, these are the real love. You? Don't know ya. *(He shoots him.)* And you?

DRAMA   I?

BEING   Yes, you.

DRAMA   Drama. The conflict within those who wish to be man, panther, lion, crow, and eagle at one and the same time.

BEING   Troublemaker! Instigator! You're here to destroy my peace of mind. To roil it all and spoil it all. By what authority? Drama, don't know ya. *(He shoots him.)* So much for all the dead weights: Good Faith, Gratitude, Senectitude, Respect for Age, Tradition, Woman, Child, Love, Drama. I'm what's left, I, the present and the future, I, the truth, I, tomorrow. Look me over. I must seek and find myself among all these skins. I am power. *(To Thôgô-gnini.)* And you. Take whichever skin you prefer. Take it before it's too late, too late.

(Monsieur Thôgô-gnini extends his hand to take the panther skin. After shooting his revolver in all directions, exit the Strange Being. The reports awaken Monsieur Thôgô-gnini.)

THÔGÔ-GNINI   Have I been asleep? Where did all these corpses come from? And this panther skin? Look, one parasite, Family, is missing. Ah, it had the good luck not to have come forward. *(He examines the corpses, reading the name identifying each of them.)* Good

Faith, Gratitude, Senectitude, Respect for Age, Tradition, Woman, Child, Love, Drama. All deservedly dead. From here on in, it's blue skies and smooth sailing.

BLACK-OUT

CURTAIN

FOURTH TABLEAU

THE STREET

(When the lights come up, the setting is a rural café. A Waiter is setting up tables. Men and Women cross the stage. A Young Woman is singing. Men are playing cards and, on occasion, arguing. A Newsboy etc. etc. Enter N'Zekou and his friend, Bouadi.)

WAITER   What will it be, gentlemen?

(N'Zekou and Bouadi look at each other and then at the Waiter.)

What will it be, gentlemen?

N'ZEKOU   A beer.

WAITER   *(to Bouadi)* And for you, sir?

BOUADI   Make mine a beer, too.

(Male and female Vendors come and go in front of the café. A Newsboy crosses the stage.)

NEWSBOY   Your "Fortune," gentlemen. Buy your "Fortune," ladies; become millionairesses, Gentlemen!

(Mademoiselle Ya-Gba crosses the stage, a cigarette in her mouth.)

N'ZEKOU   *(whistling)* Not bad!

(As Ya-Gba enters from one side, enter a blind Beggar from the other.)

BEGGAR   Give something to the Lord. To give to the poor is to have God owe you one. Have God owe you one, ladies. Show a brother compassion, gentlemen.

NEWSBOY   Your "Fortune," ladies. Become millionairesses. Gentlemen, become millionaires. Gentlemen, your "Fortune" is within your reach. Buy your "Fortune." Your "Fortune," gentlemen. *(Exit.)*

BEGGAR   Bring sunshine to my heart, gentlemen. Have God owe you one, ladies.

(Sitting at a table, Ya-Gba appears to be nervous. She looks at her watch, smokes, takes out her compact, reapplies her lipstick.)

N'ZEKOU   *(to Ya-Gba)* Will you have something with us, Mademoiselle?

YA-GBA   *(dryly)* No, Monsieur.

N'ZEKOU   Will you join us, Mademoiselle?

YA-GBA   *(ill at ease)* Thank you, no, Monsieur. *(She gets up, and, as she leaves she gives some money to the Beggar.)* For your children if you have any.

BEGGAR   May God send you many husbands!

YA-GBA   What! How's that again?

BEGGAR   May God send you long life! May God give you many children!

YA-GBA   Fine, if only He hears you.

BEGGAR   May none of your lovers ever be late for a date!

YA-GBA   *(looking him over)* Are you sure you're blind?

BEGGAR   I swear by heaven and earth I'm blind, my mother, my father, their grandparents, their great-grandparents were all blind. I come from a blind family. It's what we're famous for.

YA-GBA   And you say, you, yourself, are blind?

BEGGAR   As you can perfectly well see, I can't see you. Alms for the poor.

(Exit Ya-Gba.)

NEWSBOY   Buy your "Fortune," ladies. Become millionaires, gentlemen. Your "Fortune," gentlemen. Your "Fortune," gentlemen.

N'ZEKOU   This can't go on.

BOUADI   Huh? What can't go on?

N'ZEKOU   Conditions. Everything's falling to pieces. What used to be sure, certain, solid, isn't any more. It's all topsy-turvy.

BOUADI   Don't tell me you're against progress.

N'ZEKOU   No, you're missing the point.

BOUADI   Not at all. "This can't go on. Conditions. Everything's falling to pieces." What's to miss? Such language is scarcely cryptic.

N'ZEKOU   That beggar, for example. His family's famous for passing on handicaps rather than for shaking them off like vermin.

BOUADI   You find beggars everywhere, in Brazil, in Europe; so why not in Africa?

N'ZEKOU   It's a sign that nothing's running smoothly, that we might have the improvement there's so much room for if only we weren't in such a hurry to get rid of anything that gives life its savor and man his value.

BOUADI   That gives man his value!

N'ZEKOU   Exactly, that gives man his value. Now, I can remember when warm family ties were as constant in good times as in bad. Dropping by bright and early to ask after one another's health, I remember that.

BOUADI   Don't remember it, my friend. Won't you ever understand anything? Must you always be the pigeon? If there were no beggars, what would become of Christian charity?

N'ZEKOU   Ah, yes, charity. Their charity!

BOUADI   Now you've got it. It's a reason. *(He laughs.)* A White reason for the existence of the poor. For these Whites do nothing haphazardly. Neither do we, for that matter, but they outstrip us.

BEGGAR   To give to the poor is to have God owe you one. Have God owe you one; give to the poor. God will pay it back one day if you make it to Heaven.

BOUADI   And, if you don't make it?

BEGGAR   It will be because you haven't made God owe you one by giving enough to the poor.

BOUADI   And where will the poor go since they're in no position to have God owe them one?

BEGGAR   Unlike the rich, who're too busy to, the poor pray to God and lend the rich their excess prayers. The poor exist so the rich will appreciate their riches.

BOUADI   In other words . . .

BEGGAR   Have God owe you one, gentlemen; have God owe you one by giving to the poor.

BOUADI   (shouting) Every man for himself, and God for us all! Every man for himself!

(Reenter the Newsboy.)

NEWSBOY   Your "Fortune," gentlemen. Buy your "Fortune," gentlemen. The most widely circulated paper, the easiest reading, the most reliable source in the world. Your "Fortune!" (Exit.)

N'ZEKOU   Buy your "Fortune." It's like saying, "Buy rain. Buy wind." What a crazy idea to name a newspaper "Fortune"!

BOUADI   It's a buzz word. Every man for himself.

BEGGAR   Have God owe you one. Give to the poor. God will repay you one day soon.

BOUADI   When will he repay me?

BEGGAR   Just give without thought of anything else.

God has all the time in the world. Give. We poor have weight of numbers. Yes, we poor have weight of numbers, poor men, poor nations. On our backs, step up to paradise. From paradise on Earth to paradise in Paradise.

(Softly, a Choir is heard as if borne on the wind.)

BOUADI   Paradise in Paradise. But first comes "Every man for himself." To give to the poor is to impoverish one's self, and that's why the rich never part with a penny. A penny a day, by the end of a year, adds up to 365 pennies (366 every leap year). That's quite a bundle. 366 pennies at the current rate of exchange. It's quite a bundle, I tell you.

(Reenter the Newsboy.)

NEWSBOY   Buy your "Fortune," gentlemen. Your "Fortune," the most popular paper in the world. "Fortune"!

N'ZEKOU   Yes, indeed, that's the way to make your fortune.

BOUADI   Don't forget, my friend, that, without money, honor is merely an affliction. Money, my friend, ah, when will you grasp the fact that money makes the world go round, that, for certain men, money alone makes life worth living?

N'ZEKOU   Like Monsieur Thôgô-gnini. Umhm.

(Enter Monsieur Thôgô-gnini; sporting a Panama hat, walking stick, monocle, trousers, and a vest reaching to his knees. He is dancing with his friend, Fakron; even before sitting down, he yells out.)

THÔGÔ-GNINI   Boy! Two gins!

N'ZEKOU   *(loudly)* Unbridled license! Lies! Theft! Greed! Greee-ee-ee-eed!

THÔGÔ-GNINI   *(seated, sizing N'Zekou up)* Boy! Two gins! And snappy! Make it snappy! *(Seeing the Beggar, he laughs.)* Phony beggars.

FAKRON   He's blind.

THÔGÔ-GNINI   *(laughing)* Blind! He can see better than both of us put together. If he can find his way back home at night, he could just as easily find his way around a plantation. Ah, we mustn't deceive ourselves; we're born into a world, brought into a world where we must work, work, work ourselves to death, and, it's this working to death, this death in working that give meaning and flavor to life.

(The Boy brings the gins. Fakron laughs.)

THÔGÔ-GNINI   You're laughing, and, yet, it's the truth. Man wasn't designed for rest. Life doesn't rest; death doesn't rest. And the Good Lord, Himself, doesn't rest what with all the grievances that ascend to

Him, grievances of the rich, grievances of the poor. *(Sententiously.)* Hard work. Money.

FAKRON   *(laughing even harder)* Money, hard work! Hard work, money! My poor friend, what else is there in this world? Well, there's Man.

THÔGÔ-GNINI   *(laughing)* Man! Man, a sign his fellow men will read only if money hoists it up. I, Thôgô-gnini, am perhaps not loved, but I'm feared, respected. What's more, with total impunity, I may do as I please. Tomorrow, many among you will receive life sentences to debtors' prison. You have Monsieur Thôgô-gnini's word for that. And I'll be moving right in. I'll buy up their palm trees, their coconut groves, their peanuts. Every man for himself. *(Sententiously.)* And God for us all. *(He laughs.)* "Every man for himself," a beautiful motto to hang on façades of buildings and print on doormats of houses. And three cheers for competence and efficiency! Boy! Two gins! Ah, yes, my friend, that's how the good life of yesterday turned into a life of pure hell. In a life of pure hell, you become the Devil.

FAKRON   The Devil to frighten whom?

THÔGÔ-GNINI   The Devil has never frightened anyone. We fear him only because we know he's the Devil. We're at the moment of choice between what we had yesterday and what we'll have tomorrow. Look at me, Boy; with my monocle, my Panama hat, my walking stick, I'm the image of tomorrow. A pitiless tomorrow.

A monocle so as to see with only one eye, enormous appetite, enormous thirst. (*He downs the glass of gin in one gulp.*) Whew! Boy, another gin!

(*The Boy brings the gin.*)

Another chair. This one's getting too small for me.

(*They bring him an armchair.*)

How good it is to take it easy . . . to fill up a chair, to be aware of one's worth. That's what sufficiency means.

(*Reenter Ya-Gba, but, seeing Thôgô-gnini with Fakron, exit.*)

FAKRON You're certainly brimming with ideas.

THÔGÔ-GNINI By now, I understand life. (*To the Boy.*) Boy, are you content with your lot?

BOY (*surprised*) With my lot?

THÔGÔ-GNINI Yes, with your lot?

BOY What lot?

THÔGÔ-GNINI Why, the lot of a boy.

BOY Oh, the lot of a boy. I couldn't be more content. I get to do a lot of listening and to observe everything.

I've come to the conclusion that what's emerging is a class of White Blacks who, for one thing, declaim, "Every man for himself, and God for us all!".

FAKRON *(laughing)* "Every man for himself." Are those the new buzz words?

BOY Everyone aims at being the brightest star in the darkest sky, and my third observation is that this class is short of patience, long on greed, and brutal. Ah, if the ancient Africans could rise from their graves, they wouldn't recognize us, and they'd wonder whether we Blacks weren't on the point of losing not only our Blackness but also our talent for laughter.

THÔGÔ-GNINI These are scarcely times for laughter; these are times for keeping your eyes open. It's good that Blacks no longer know how to laugh.

FAKRON The kings of Europe study the Black man in order to learn how to laugh. Today, the Black man is abandoning laughter. Tomorrow, he'll have to hire Europeans to teach him to laugh as before.

THÔGÔ-GNINI *(laughing)* Let's not exaggerate. Professors of laughter and consultants on the technique of laughter, come now!

FAKRON Nevertheless, the way things are going, it's not impossible. Every man for himself. An end to living in harmony, to wishing one another well, to thinking of anybody else. In the end, seeing only yourself erodes both sleep and laughter.

THÔGÔ-GNINI   (laughing) These experts would have to be of surpassing excellence for the laughter to be neither noisy nor sarcastic nor bitter nor childish nor insane nor, and this is the most crucial, of any discernible color. God sees to it that the laughter we learn is neither yellow nor green nor blue nor red.

FAKRON   When we've lost our beautiful Black laughter, may our professors teach us human laughter in golden mouths!

THÔGÔ-GNINI   (laughing) A fine prayer that is! A silver mouth, a golden mouth, a diamond mouth! On you, on me, on everybody? If it weren't for silver and such, there'd have been no Judas; there'd be no turncoats; there'd be no turndashikis. The expressions, "have nations," "have-not nations," the words, "currency," "money," "pound," "dollar," "gourde," "franc," "ruble," these words, these expressions would never have come into being. Silver enriches language as well as men. Boy! Two gins!

(Reenter the Newsboy.)

NEWSBOY   Your "Fortune"! Buy your "Fortune," gentlemen, your "Fortune"! Your "Fortune," gentlemen, the most popular paper in the world, the largest circulation in the world.

29

BEGGAR Give to the poor; have God owe you one. The rich who give to the poor will pass through the eye of the needle to see God face to face.

THÔGÔ-GNINI Boy, do you have friends?

BOY Friends?

THÔGÔ-GNINI Yes, friends. My meaning's clear. Friends.

BOY Friends! Friends? Nowadays, can anyone tell who's a friend and who's an enemy? Does anyone know what law governs men and nations now that the Whites have invaded our citadel with their palm-oil rigmarole?

THÔGÔ-GNINI Palm-oil. (*He laughs.*) Go on.

BOY Can anyone determine what a man is worth or what safeguards he has when he, in the name of the king, is subject to arrest at any hour of the day or night on the slightest pretext?

THÔGÔ-GNINI Watch it, Boy. You'd better learn what not to say.

BOY You don't understand, Monsieur Thôgô-gnini; everyone's terrified of you. Your name makes even the children tremble.

THÔGÔ-GNINI It's good that everyone's terrified of

Monsieur Thôgô-gnini. It's proof of their respect.

BOY   Everyone's terrified of Monsieur Thôgô-gnini, and muggers and swindlers.

THÔGÔ-GNINI   (*striking him with his walking stick*) That will do! That will do!

BEGGAR   Think of us who have weight of numbers. The weight of the world rests on us. Give to the poor . . . to the true roots of society. Have God owe you one by giving to the poor.

   (*Suddenly a strong wind begins blowing bringing in its wake leaves and bank notes. Thôgô-gnini and Fakron rush to pick up the bank notes, vying for them with the Newsboy and with the Beggar, who threatens them with his staff.*)

N'ZEKOU   (*with jeering laughter*) All hail beggars, newsboys, scuzz! Hail! I say, "Hail, scuzz!" (*He laughs.*) How good it is to fill up a chair! How good it is to contend with beggars! That's what sufficiency means! (*He laughs.*)

THÔGÔ-GNINI   (*realizing he is N'Zekou's laughing-stock*) Repeat that to my face if you're a man.

N'ZEKOU   A man! Well, I have all the attributes, all the characteristics.

THÔGÔ-GNINI   Not quite enough. Prove you're a man by repeating what you've just said.

N'ZEKOU   What I've just said? What did you hear? What you heard is what I've just said.

THÔGÔ-GNINI   *(angrily)* You don't know me yet. I'm the panther man . . . . As for you, you're a zero; you stand for nothing. Nothing, do you hear? I'm the one who's a man, a somebody, a big name. I'm Monsieur Thôgô-gnini, Monsieur Thôgô-gnini, Monsieur Thôgô-gnini. *(Exit.)*

(Loud police whistles. Enter at top speed Policemen wearing the uniforms the Trader had distributed during the First Tableau.)

FIRST POLICEMAN   *(billy club in hand)* What're you up to?

N'ZEKOU   I'm out for a stroll.

POLICEMAN   Go stroll some place else.

N'ZEKOU   Some place else? Why?

POLICEMAN   Why? There doesn't have to be any why. That's how it goes. *(He shoves N'Zekou.)*

N'ZEKOU   Don't shove me.

POLICEMAN   Get going and now! Get going! *(He shoves N'Zekou, who resists.)* You're looking for trouble? You obstruct an officer in the performance of his duty? You set yourself up against the law? Well, we'll see about that!

N'ZEKOU   Don't shove me.

POLICEMAN   Who are you?

N'ZEKOU   Who am I? I'm a man.

POLICEMAN   Man or not, move it! *(Pushing N'Zekou, the Policeman blows his whistle. Enter two more Policemen.)* Arrest him for resisting an arresting officer, for insulting the same officer, for disturbing the peace, for a subversive, seditious attitude, and worst of all, for refusing to move it, re-fu-sing to move it.

(The Policemen take N'Zekou away. We next see a procession of Unfortunates behind bars. Following one another are a grinning Old Man, a smiling Child, a weeping Woman, and N'Zekou shaking the bars and shouting.)

N'ZEKOU   Air! Light! Space, gentlemen! Life, gentlemen! Ah, Thôgô-gnini! Monsieur Thôgô-gnini!

(Bird songs, sweet music. The bars give. Exit N'Zekou roaring with anger.)

Ah, Thôgô-gnini! Thôgô-gnini! Thôgô-gnini!

CURTAIN

FIFTH TABLEAU

MONSIEUR THÔGÔ-GNINI'S ESTABLISHMENT

(Monsieur Thôgô-gnini's office, a hut with big red letters reading "MONSIEUR THÔGÔ-GNINI: MAKING MONEY'S MY LINE." The office adjoins a bedroom. On the table, a teapot, cups, sugar, and files in racks and cases. It is morning. Wearing a dressing gown and a nightcap, Monsieur Thôgô-gnini is drinking tea with Ya-Gba.)

THÔGÔ-GNINI *(drinking)* My child, how good it is to be alive, to see the sun again each day, to get up in the morning to take tea.

YA-GBA It smells good, this tea.

THÔGÔ-GNINI It's imported from China.

YA-GBA Just think of importing tea from China, of drinking tea from China on African shores.

THÔGÔ-GNINI Only Monsieur Thôgô-gnini is in such a position. Being somebody, being a world-class celebrity brings certain privileges with it.

YA-GBA Your reputation's solidly established. Everyone knows who Monsieur Thôgô-gnini is and where his establishment is. If it weren't for you, what would become of the king?

THÔGÔ-GNINI   More important, if it weren't for me, what would become of the country? It's because of me that every ship in the world comes to our port. The businessmen know no one but me, Monsieur Thôgô-gnini. But being rich in a poor land means problems pile up. I made my fortune honestly, completely honestly.

YA-GBA   We know. Palm oil.

THÔGÔ-GNINI   To get it, I had to work, work hard, to go for days without sleep, for nights without sleep, for years without sleep. I'm a self-made man. There's no one I owe, no one.

YA-GBA   We know, Monsieur Thôgô-gnini.

THÔGÔ-GNINI   I've about had a bellyfull of what they're saying about me.

YA-GBA   No, the rich, like the high and mighty, must accept criticism. And accepting criticism makes them look good with the added bonus that it doesn't prevent them from doing as they please.

THÔGÔ-GNINI   You're right, of course, my child. Still, the people's ingratitude was getting to be more than I could take.

YA-GBA   Think of only the nation, Monsieur Thôgô-gnini, of only the nation.

THÔGÔ-GNINI   What would become of it without
me? And that's why, for Monsieur Thôgô-gnini, it's
"once more into the breach." You'll have to leave, my
dear. It's time for me to get to work. And to think they
call me greedy. Happily, you understand, my dear. Go
out the back way; here's the key.

   (Exit Ya-Gba.)

What's left for me to get my hands on? I already have
the rice, the cotton, and the tobacco monopolies, the
oil and the banana monopolies, the ginger, the ivory,
and the copra monopolies as well as the . . . . (He
laughs.) It's good to be alive. (He turns around to see
N'Zekou who has entered.) You? And here so early?
What do you want?

N'ZEKOU   (calmly) You know perfectly well.

THÔGÔ-GNINI   No. How could I? I'm not a mind
reader.

N'ZEKOU   (calmly) I've come to collect what you owe
me.

THÔGÔ-GNINI   (feigning surprise) What I owe you?
(As if trying to place it.) What I owe you? Rather it's the
rest of you who owe me everything. Come on now. Be
reasonable. You are because I am, because I exist.
O.K.? O.K.?

N'ZEKOU   No, it's too easy to pretend to forget. It's two years now that you've refused to pay me for twenty casks of palm oil.

THÔGÔ-GNINI   *(laughing)* Two years! Two years! It takes a prodigious memory to recall after two years that you still owe a bill for twenty casks of palm oil. Then again, what palm oil are we talking about? I can't place it for the life of me.

N'ZEKOU   You can't place it?

THÔGÔ-GNINI   Not for the life of me, no. There must be some mistake. You've confused me with someone else. I've never done business with you.

N'ZEKOU   *(shocked)* Really, never? You don't recall transacting with me for twenty casks of palm oil two years ago? *(Taking out a paper.)* And this paper, this paper, do you recognize it?

THÔGÔ-GNINI   Give it here.

N'ZEKOU   *(warily)* Look, but don't touch.

THÔGÔ-GNINI   How can I examine it to verify it if you won't give me the paper?

N'ZEKOU   *(holding it up to his eyes)* This signature, then? Do you recognize *it*, at least? This sig-na-ture?

THÔGÔ-GNINI   I can't see anything up so close.

N'ZEKOU   (moving the paper farther away) Do you recognize this sig-na-ture?

THÔGÔ-GNINI   (phlegmatically) No.

N'ZEKOU   No?

THÔGÔ-GNINI   No.

(Standing with his arms crossed, N'Zekou looks him up and down.)

You may look me up and down all you want to, I'll still say "No." (He laughs.) If you're planning to trick me, you have to get up early in the morning. I sleep with one eye open.

N'ZEKOU   Yet this paper, this signature are still here.

THÔGÔ-GNINI   (apodeictically) This paper's phony.

N'ZEKOU   What!

THÔGÔ-GNINI   Phony.

N'ZEKOU   Phony?

THÔGÔ-GNINI   Authentically phony.

N'ZEKOU   (*showing the paper as he approaches Thôgô-gnini*) This is phony? This signature, phony? Come on, Thôgô-gnini.

THÔGÔ-GNINI   (*calmly*) Monsieur Thôgô-gnini.

N'ZEKOU   Thieves don't deserve such courtesy.

THÔGÔ-GNINI   (*laughing*) Monsieur Thôgô-gnini, it's required.

N'ZEKOU   (*contemptuously*) Monsieur Thôgô-gnini.

THÔGÔ-GNINI   (*after sitting down*) Ah, now I'll listen.

N'ZEKOU   Monsieur Thôgô-gnini, you're a crook.

THÔGÔ-GNINI   Please don't make phrases. So you're here to cheat me! (*With irony.*) Twenty casks of palm oil two years ago. Now look me in the eye. I wasn't born yesterday. I've been in business thirty years, and no one's ever gotten the best of me. I've got backbone, lots of backbone.

N'ZEKOU   Crook, thief!

THÔGÔ-GNINI   Calm yourself. Twenty casks of palm oil. Two years ago. And it's only this morning you suddenly remember the debt. You must have had sweet dreams last night, my friend.

N'ZEKOU   God, save us from trash like Thôgô-gnini!

THÔGÔ-GNINI   (*getting up, he steps forward swiftly snatching the paper from the hands of N'Zekou and tearing it up as he shouts at the top of his voice*) The game is up! Here's how I deal with your twenty casks of palm oil! I've salted the money away. It's here. (*Indicating his pocket.*) Take your complaints to whomever you please.

(*N'Zekou moves toward Thôgô-gnini.*)

Take your complaints wherever you like.

N'ZEKOU   Thôgô-gnini.

THÔGÔ-GNINI   Monsieur Thôgô-gnini.

N'ZEKOU   Monsieur Thôgô-gnini.

THÔGÔ-GNINI   In the flesh, now and forever. Monsieur Thôgô-gnini, the man who never pardons any offense.

N'ZEKOU   (*scornfully*) Monsieur Thôgô-gnini. (*Moving toward him.*) Old crook! Thief! And that's what's serving as the king's cane-bearer. If the king knew what he had in his employ . . . .

THÔGÔ-GNINI   The king! The king! He knows everything. He knows perfectly well with whom he's dealing. I took a mere twenty casks of oil from you! You're lucky it wasn't the fifty, the hundred I've taken from others. A hundred casks of oil that I don't mind saying will never be paid for. Never! Ah, you obviously don't know Monsieur Thôgô-gnini. The very idea of moving Heaven and Earth over twenty casks of oil. What's the world coming to? What winds of madness are whisking the world away? (*To N'Zekou.*) What winds of madness are whisking you away?

N'ZEKOU   No, I'm not mad. I'm in the know.

THÔGÔ-GNINI   I'll speak to the king this very evening about your seditious ideas. I'll go into detail, do you hear, into detail? To dare come insult me, Monsieur Thôgô-gnini, in my own establishment, my own establishment. What's happened to respect? And what will be next? To dare violate the residence of Monsieur Thôgô-gnini?

N'ZEKOU   I'm in the know. Everyone's in the know. Everyone but the king.

THÔGÔ-GNINI   What? What's that you're saying?

N'ZEKOU   The king doesn't know that you've grabbed all the hunting lands for yourself, all the best land. The fishing industry? You've reserved exclusively for yourself all the streams where fish are plentiful, and the richest forests as well. The king doesn't know any of this.

THÔGÔ-GNINI   Silence!

N'ZEKOU   The king doesn't know you've defiled women, corrupted men, arranged for the murders of Wangara businessmen, of stubborn Hausa vendors. And what happened to the property of those seamen found dead one morning in their cabin?

THÔGÔ-GNINI   Silence! Be still!

N'ZEKOU   Yes, Monsieur Thôgô-gnini, we've got a whole lot on you. If you sleep with one eye open, we don't sleep at all. The day will come —

THÔGÔ-GNINI   So you don't sleep. You spy on me, eh! You pray for my death, the death of Monsieur Thôgô-gnini. *(He laughs.)* It's not set for tomorrow, nor the day after. What could you blab about Monsieur Thôgô-gnini? You poor fool, nothing!

N'ZEKOU   Nothing? We could tell the king you've surrounded him with a pack of agents who spy on him night and day, and that you purposely keep him in the dark, that you're dipping with both hands into the royal exchequer, that he's the one whose picking up the tab for your extravagances and your so-called generosities.

THÔGÔ-GNINI   Enough!

N'ZEKOU   Incidentally, what's with your conspiracy to dethrone him?

THÔGÔ-GNINI   Enough! This is too much for even my great forbearance. Isn't there anyone who appreciates my selfless striving? Is there nothing but ingratitude? But things won't go on like this. Oh, no, I swear they won't. For the first time, I'm going to be implacable.

N'ZEKOU   For the first time! Pig! Thief! (*Moving toward him.*) Gangster! Slaver!

THÔGÔ-GNINI   (*in a panic*) Help! Help! Murder! Murder! Boy! Boy!

   (*Enter Policemen.*)

Get him out of here! Get this thing out of here! . . . . Wait a minute. (*Fearfully, Thôgô-gnini creeps up to N'Zekou and says to his face:*) You poor fool. (*He loses his balance, falls, gets up, and returns to his chair. Exeunt the Policemen with N'Zekou.*)

At last, I'm rid of that one. He's a toughie. Ah, that was a rough one! But another score's been settled. (*He sits down.*) A conspiracy against the king, Wangara businessmen, murdered seamen! What kind of times are we living in? I'm going to have to speak to the king, take the bull by the horns. Oh, that N'Zekou, that N'Zekou! He just might turn out to be a problem. It's a good thing I'm Monsiur Thôgô-gnini that defiler of women, that corrupter of men! A conspiracy against the King! He shouldn't live another day.

(Enter a Servant.)

SERVANT   Monsieur, two White men would like to see you.

THÔGÔ-GNINI   Two White men? What are they like?

SERVANT   White.

THÔGÔ-GNINI   Show them in.

(Exit the Servant. Enter two White Men carrying valises.)

BOTH WHITE MEN   Greetings, Monsieur Thôgô-gnini.

THÔGÔ-GNINI   Oh, it's you. Greetings, greetings. *(He shakes hands with them.)* Greetings, welcome. Sit down.

ELDER WHITE MAN   We've brought you some beautiful things from civilization.

THÔGÔ-GNINI   Sit down. Please sit down. Sitting down with a composed mind is the only way to talk business. Make yourselves comfortable. May I offer you something?

BOTH WHITE MEN   Certainly. Yes, indeed. That would just hit the spot.

THÔGÔ-GNINI Boy, Boy, bring us something to drink. It's been years since you've been here. Much too long. I've run out of merchandise; there's nothing left to sell. You've arrived in the nick of time.

YOUNGER WHITE MAN It's a long trip. The winds aren't always favorable. To your health.

THÔGÔ-GNINI (*taking a healthy swig*) Now let's talk shop. For two years, business has been booming. Palm oil, peanuts, copra . . . . What have you brought me?

(*The elder White Man opens the valises to display for Thôgô-gnini glassware, cloth, beverages, hardware, all sorts of trumpery, to each of which, he points with pride.*)

ELDER WHITE MAN (*showing Thôgô-gnini a suit made of gunnysacks*) What a suit I've brought you! The most beautiful fabric being made in Europe today, the fabric anybody who is anybody is wearing. An exclusive fabric. We've had it made to order especially for you. Just wait till you try it on.

THÔGÔ-GNINI Yes, yes, I want to try it on right now. (*He puts the suit on and struts back and forth modeling it.*)

ELDER WHITE MAN The finest fabric in the world. And one you'll find nowhere on the shores of either East or West Africa. This garment was designed especially for you as a nonpareil type. A man on a par with the kings of Europe.

46

(Thôgô-gnini, still strutting up and down, nods his approval.)

THÔGÔ-GNINI   On a par with the kings of Europe. What an honor! How does the suit suit me?

YOUNGER WHITE MAN   That suit is you. The ladies won't have a chance.

THÔGÔ-GNINI   No, that's all behind me.

YOUNGER WHITE MAN   You're lucky. Where we come from, it's nothing like that. Every springtime it's flowers — and women. Ah, springtime back home.

THÔGÔ-GNINI   How I wish I could wear this suit in your country!

YOUNGER WHITE MAN   You'd be a sensation, an absolute sensation. Come visit us! Do come visit us! You'll see for yourself how delightful our lifestyle is and how bountifully our temperate climate treats us.

THÔGÔ-GNINI   I long to visit your country, your beautiful country! In anticipation of that happy day, may I ask you a favor?

YOUNGER WHITE MAN   Ask. Why not?

THÔGÔ-GNINI   I'd like to have a mass said in memory of my father who died some years ago.

YOUNGER WHITE MAN *(astonished)* A memorial mass in Europe for your father who died in Africa.

THÔGÔ-GNINI Yes.

YOUNGER WHITE MAN But nobody knew him over there.

THÔGÔ-GNINI Certainly, God knew him, and, whether here or there, a mass, once said in his name, will remain his mass.

YOUNGER WHITE MAN Of course, of course, but still . . . .

THÔGÔ-GNINI And, yes, I must confess he died before being washed whiter than snow.

YOUNGER WHITE MAN Whiter than snow.

THÔGÔ-GNINI By baptism . . . and —

YOUNGER WHITE MAN *(interrupting him)* God doesn't scruple about color; He sounds only the human heart.

THÔGÔ-GNINI Now that we've established friendly relations, I'd like your God to welcome my father (who never knew Him) into His Kingdom. I must have an eye to the future.

YOUNGER WHITE MAN   Oh, I get it. Monsieur Thôgô-gnini — even in the eyes of the Good Lord.

THÔGÔ-GNINI   (laughing) Monsieur Thôgô-gnini must remain Monsieur Thôgô-gnini even in the eyes of the Good Lord.

YOUNGER WHITE MAN   But to have a mass said in so distant a land.

THÔGÔ-GNINI   They must become aware over in your country no less than in Heaven that, on these African shores, is one Monsieur Thôgô-gnini, a man of great eminence. If my name becomes part of your history, the next step is eternity . . . eternity.

YOUNGER WHITE MAN   I'll take these matters up with my king as soon as I get back home.

THÔGÔ-GNINI   (happy) To live in the memory of White men is really to have lived! I'm going to be immortal. But that's not quite enough. I'd like something more. A street named after me . . . named after Monsieur Thôgô-gnini.

YOUNGER WHITE MAN   Nothing's impossible. That, too, might be easily arranged.

THÔGÔ-GNINI   I'm sure it would come high.

YOUNGER WHITE MAN   Extremely high. In this

world, however, anything is for sale if the price is right.

THÔGÔ-GNINI   Well, let me think about it.

YOUNGER WHITE MAN   Give it a lot of thought.

THÔGÔ-GNINI   Oh, a whole lot, especially if it will be an expense.

YOUNGER WHITE MAN   A great big expense.

THÔGÔ-GNINI   Couldn't they do them for nothing?

YOUNGER WHITE MAN   Do what for nothing?

THÔGÔ-GNINI   The mass and the name of the street.

YOUNGER WHITE MAN   I'll speak to my king, Monsieur Thôgô-gnini. Wait a minute. Now that I think of it, it would be a simple matter to give your name to backwoods comfort stations.

THÔGÔ-GNINI   (happy) Give my name to backwoods comfort stations!

YOUNGER WHITE MAN   In France, these little structures are called "vespasiennes;" so your name would be replacing that of a celebrated Roman emperor.

THÔGÔ-GNINI   (in seventh heaven) My name in place of a celebrated Roman emperor's! What an imperial way to break into history!

YOUNGER WHITE MAN   Your name will be engraved on the pure white porcelain of the comfort stations.

THÔGÔ-GNINI   *(ecstatic)* My name engraved on the pure white porcelain of backwoods comfort stations! The name of Monsieur Thôgô-gnini engraved on pure white porcelain in the boondocks! Eternal thanks to your gods who have made me what I am today! I'm going to be the most important man in Africa. For centuries, for millenia, my name on the pure white porcelain of comfort stations will defy the erosion of time. They'll go on talking about me; they'll go on recounting my triumphs, the triumphs of Thôgô-gnini, Thôgô-gnini, Thôgô . . . . *(To the younger white man.)* Just what is a comfort station?

YOUNGER WHITE MAN   A little structure for men in urgent need.

THÔGÔ-GNINI   Oh, a little structure for men in urgent need. Just a little structure. Well, what does it matter? For an entry into eternity, any route will do. I, at least, shall have robbed no man of his freedom, shall have shed no man's blood, but, with spotless hands, shall enter immortality by the imperial pathway of the comfort station. Bless the gods, and praise their names!

YOUNGER WHITE MAN   One small matter. Your name, it's a bit too common to rub shoulders with those of the greats of our land, who, when you come down to it, are great sticklers for protocol. For you, obviously, they'll overlook certain irregularities, but they'll have to comply with the rules ór, at least, with some minimum of correctitude so that no one will get the idea that just anything goes. In the final analysis, rank does have its privileges.

THÔGÔ-GNINI   (*saddened*) But . . . what name?

(*The two White Men pretend to ponder the question.*)

Suggest something.

YOUNGER WHITE MAN.   For example, you might be Monsieur Thôgô-gnini van Africa . . . ben Tropics.

THÔGÔ-GNINI   Monsieur Thôgô-gnini van Africa ben Trafficker?

YOUNGER WHITE MAN   That's even better. We could make it Monsieur Thôgô-gnini van Africa ben Trafficker de Benin.

THÔGÔ-GNINI   Monsieur Thôgô-gnini van Africa ben Trafficker de Benin and all that on the pure white porcelain of boondocks comfort stations! You're sent from Heaven. But they also call me the panther.

YOUNGER WHITE MAN   The panther?

THÔGÔ-GNINI   It's like a wolf, only African.

YOUNGER WHITE MAN   Hmm. "Panther." Better and better. Then we'd have Monsieur Thôgô, the Gnini of Panther van Africa ben Trafficker de Benin.

THÔGÔ-GNINI   Monsieur Thôgô, the Gnini of Panther van Africa ben Trafficker de Benin. Thank you, gentlemen. (*He shakes their hands.*) Thank you again.

YOUNGER WHITE MAN   Your Lordship of Panther, it's getting late. When may we see you again to go over the books?

THÔGÔ-GNINI   Why, tomorrow, to be sure.

BOTH WHITE MEN   (*drinking*) To your health and prosperity, Monsieur Thôgô-gnini.

THÔGÔ-GNINI   (*drinking*) Thank you! Thank you! To our continued collaboration! To our friendship!

BOTH WHITE MEN   (*as they leave*) Till tomorrow then, Monsieur Thôgô-gnini.

THÔGÔ-GNINI   Yes, till tomorrow, tomorrow.

(*Exeunt the two White Men. Admiringly, Monsieur Thôgô-gnini examines the contents of the valises.*)

I'm going to do well. Make lots of money!

(Reenter the Servant.)

SERVANT   Monsieur, there's a woman to see you.

THÔGÔ-GNINI   *(returning the merchandise to the valises)* A woman to see me? A woman?

SERVANT   Yes.

THÔGÔ-GNINI   What's she like?

SERVANT   Quite beautiful!

THÔGÔ-GNINI   *(checking his appearance)* You're sure, now?

SERVANT   *(laughing)* Quite, quite beautiful!

THÔGÔ-GNINI   Show her in! Show her in!

   (Enter Brouba.)

Come in, Madam. Come in. Sit down, Madam. Make yourself at home, Madam.

BROUBA   I prefer to stand.

THÔGÔ-GNINI   No, Madam. In Monsieur Thôgô-gnini's establishment, sitting down's the rule, especially for beautiful women like you. So sit down, Madam.

(Brouba sits down. Thôgô-gnini sits next to her.)

Now what may I do for you, Madam?

BROUBA   I'm looking for my brother.

THÔGÔ-GNINI   *(surprised)* Looking for your brother! Who's your brother?

BROUBA   N'Zekou.

THÔGÔ-GNINI   Which N'Zekou?

BROUBA   N'Zekou Paul.

THÔGÔ-GNINI   Oh, N'Zekou Paul is your brother, is he?

BROUBA   Yes, he's my brother.

THÔGÔ-GNINI   What a pity a woman as lovely, as charming as you has to be the sister of a gutter rat, a crook.

BROUBA   Thôgô-gnini!

THÔGÔ-GNINI   Monsieur Thôgô-gnini.

BROUBA   Monsieur Thôgô-gnini.

THÔGÔ-GNINI   Yes, your brother tried to swindle me

by means of a fraudulent claim to . . . I forget how much.

BROUBA   He was telling the truth, Monsieur Thôgô-gnini, the truth.

THÔGÔ-GNINI   What do you mean "the truth"?

BROUBA   Yes, the absolute truth. I was the one who reminded him of the transaction this morning.

THÔGÔ-GNINI   You, Madam?

BROUBA   I, Monsieur Thôgô-gnini.

THÔGÔ-GNINI   All I can say is it's the worst notion that's ever come into your head, Madam.

BROUBA   What's that?

THÔGÔ-GNINI   (moving closer) All the same, it's nothing serious. With women, always a little latitude, a little indulgence especially when they're as charming as you and when . . . and when . . . .

BROUBA   And when . . . and when . . . and when?

THÔGÔ-GNINI   And when . . . and when . . . you take my meaning. You women are so clever, so intuitive.

56

BROUBA   No, forgive me, but I don't take your meaning.

THÔGÔ-GNINI   How can I put it into words? Er . . . er . . . . You're gorgeous, you know. I've never met a woman half so bewitching as you. I'm totally befuddled. Call me Thôgô-gnini, just Thôgô-gnini.

BROUBA   Monsieur Thôgô-gnini.

THÔGÔ-GNINI   No, no, no, no, Madam. For you, it's Thôgô-gnini.

BROUBA   Monsieur Thôgô-gnini is not too much trouble. And you haven't answered my question.

THÔGÔ-GNINI   I haven't answered the lady's question. Ah, how can I make it explicit? Make it explicit that . . . that . . . . Place your hand on my heart, Madam, and then you'll understand. (He sighs.) Ah, if only you wished to understand.

BROUBA   Be more direct, Monsieur Thôgô-gnini. We women like clear, precise statements and honorable dealings.

THÔGÔ-GNINI   Honorable dealings?

BROUBA   Yes, Monsieur Thôgô-gnini, honorable dealings.

THÔGÔ-GNINI   (*repulsed*) So Madam doesn't take my
meaning. Well the meaning Madam doesn't take is how
immediately she must vacate the premises and how
little business Paul N'Zekou's sister has being in the
house of Monsieur Thôgô-gnini.

BROUBA   Monsieur Thôgô-gnini.

THÔGÔ-GNINI   None of your Monsieur Thôgô-
gnini's. Just get out, get out, get out, Madam!

BROUBA   Thôgô-gnini.

THÔGÔ-GNINI   No, Monsieur Thôgô-gnini! Monsieur Thôgô-gnini, Madam.

BROUBA   Compose yourself, Monsieur Thôgô-gnini,
compose youself. We're the ones who ought to be in a
rage, we who've been harmed, we who've been robbed.

THÔGÔ-GNINI   Robbed! Robbed!

BROUBA   Yes, robbed. You know and know well what
misery you've sown around you. You know and know
well whom you've thrown out into the street, women,
old men, children . . . .

THÔGÔ-GNINI   (*laughing*) Women, old men, children.

BROUBA   Yes, that's right, laugh, laugh. We've

learned the meanings of hunger, cold, poverty, making do with nothing. We've learned the meanings of an empty pot, a bare hearth with children beside it weeping with hunger and shivering with cold — and who finally starve to death beside the bare hearth. Ah, Thôgô-gnini!

THÔGÔ-GNINI   Monsieur Thôgô-gnini.

BROUBA   Ah, Monsieur Thôgô-gnini.

THÔGÔ-GNINI   *(laughing)* Children starving to death.

BROUBA   There are thousands of us whom you've victimized, Monsieur Thôgô-gnini, thousands. Do you hear, thousands?

THÔGÔ-GNINI   Thousands, you say? And how many thousands? *(He laughs.)*

BROUBA   You're a monster, a monster!

THÔGÔ-GNINI   A monster! Get out of my house, Madam. Get out of my house!

BROUBA   *(firmly)* No, I refuse to go. I demand to know what's happened to my brother. I demand to know.

THÔGÔ-GNINI   You'll learn nothing from me. Get out!

BROUBA   No, I'm not going.

THÔGÔ-GNINI   We'll see about that. Boy! Boy!

(Reenter Servant, followed by others.)

This lady won't take my meaning. This lady won't get
out. Take her away! Drag her out of here!

BROUBA   *(shouting)* Monster! Coward! Scumbag!
Thief!

(Exeunt the Boys dragging Brouba with them.)

THÔGÔ-GNINI   Oh, what a world! And what a family! You can't live in peace any more. Not in this country
of . . . types who wake you up at dawn for nonsense like
paying your debts that date back two years, two years!
But I'm finally rid of that riffraff who's trying to pass
herself off as an honest woman, an honorable woman,
as a paragon of virtue — self-styled. Ah, you're the one,
Thôgô-gnini . . . er, Monsieur Thôgô-gnini; you're
magnificient, Monsieur Thôgô-gnini. You're great,
Monsieur Thôgô-gnini; you're the greatest.

*(Enter three Toughs as Thôgô-gnini struts about in his
suit.)*

What do you want? Who are you?

(The first Tough pulls out a long knife and, by placing his index finger on his lips, orders Thôgô-gnini to be silent. The second Tough shows Thôgô-gnini a club and signals him to sit down. Moving back a few steps, Thôgô-gnini falls into the chair. The third Tough makes Thôgô-gnini open his mouth wider and wider.)

FIRST TOUGH   *(raising his knife and striking Thôgô-gnini in the teeth with it)* Panther teeth. Shark's teeth. Let's have a good look at those teeth. A better look than that.

(The third Tough gags Thôgô-gnini, ties his hands, whitens his face, reddens his lips with lipstick, puts neck-laces around his neck and earrings into his ears.)

FIRST TOUGH   *(knife still drawn)* Dance!

(Thôgô-gnini dances while the two other Toughs ransack the place for money. They find some in a drawer. They present the odor of the money for Thôgô-gnini to smell. Then they tie him to the chair after sticking a sign reading "Every man for himself" to his chest. Exeunt taking the valises and their contents with them. Shortly afterward, reenter the Servant, who, seeing Thôgô-gnini tied up, runs away screaming. Enter a Woman who similarly runs away screaming, for no one recognizes Thôgô-gnini in his new getup. Some Men run in, remove the gag, and untie Thôgô-gnini, who begins to weep.)

THÔGÔ-GNINI   My money! My money! My money!

THE OTHERS   *(imitating him)* His money! His money!

CURTAIN

SIXTH TABLEAU

THE TRIAL

(In Africa, trials are taking on the characteristics of those of Europe. The results of this creeping influence are visible here. A presiding Judge in robes and wearing a red revolutionary cap, a bald Court Clerk with bushy whiskers and an old bowlegged Usher in evening clothes with a chain half-way down his leg. Some Persons under a lean-to. The clanking of chains.)

JUDGE   Next case.

CLERK   Usher, bring the accused, N'Zekou.

USHER   Prisoner N'Zekou! N'Zekou.

(Enter N'Zekou in the custody of a fat Policeman with a curlicue mustache, a rifle in his bandolier, a quirt in his hand. N'Zekou is in chains. The chain starts at his feet, goes up to encircle his waist and then his shoulders. The Policeman holds the end of the chain.)

JUDGE   You again!

N'ZEKOU   I again, Your Honor.

JUDGE   Do you do it for fun?

N'ZEKOU   No, Your Honor, but it's certainly fun for some others I could mention.

JUDGE   When all is said and done, the underlying cause must be serious.

N'ZEKOU   Underlying causes are always easy enough to discover, Your Honor.

JUDGE   What do you mean?

N'ZEKOU   Nothing as of now, Your Honor. My time to speak has not yet come.

JUDGE   Let's get on with it. You must know the procedure.

N'ZEKOU   By heart, Your Honor.

JUDGE   State your name and —

N'ZEKOU   N'Zekou Paul Latoux Bravho, born in 1820, son of Latoux Brahvo Gnongnon and Coubra Marie Toutouka, both deceased. Married, seven children, all living, address: Prison.

JUDGE   What did you say? "Prison"?

N'ZEKOU   Yes, address: Prison.

JUDGE   Your family lives somewhere in this city.

N'ZEKOU   I no longer know where they live. I've lost touch.

JUDGE   Come now, let's not exaggerate. Not everyone is a prisoner even when one takes into account the exiguity of the landmass, the immensity of the oceans, the inexorable advance of the desert . . . .

N'ZEKOU   I, myself, never take into account the exiguity of the landmass. I am, in plain words, in prison or, to be more explicit, in the confinement of prison. I am the prisoner of Monsieur Thôgô-gnini. I am the court jester of Monsieur Thôgô-gnini. I am the pet aversion of Monsieur Thôgô-gnini.

JUDGE   What are you saying?

N'ZEKOU   I'm saying "the prisoner of Monsieur Thôgô-gnini."

(The chains keep up a constant rattle.)

JUDGE   Silence in court.

N'ZEKOU   It's the chain that's talking.

JUDGE   What chain?

N'ZEKOU   My chain.

JUDGE   *(commandingly)* It must be still.

(The rattling continues.)

Do you understand?

N'ZEKOU   Yes, Your Honor, it's still.

(The Assemblage heaves a sign of relief for the silence.)

JUDGE   Why were you arrested?

N'ZEKOU   Because I'd come to Monsieur Thôgô-gnini to ask him to pay me for twenty casks of palm oil.

JUDGE   *(slowly)* To ask Monsieur Thôgô-gnini to pay you for twenty casks of palm oil.

N'ZEKOU   Yes, Your Honor.

JUDGE   Is that sufficient reason to arrest anybody?

N'ZEKOU   Maybe not, but it's the best I can do.

JUDGE   Obviously. All the same, you knew who Monsieur Thôgô-gnini was. So why offer him provocation?

N'ZEKOU   Is it provocation to seek the payment of a debt?

JUDGE   There are those who believe in no debts but those owed to them. Monsieur Thôgô-gnini is of that kidney. Besides, that's not the formal charge.

66

N'ZEKOU   Your Honor, by now, I'm quite inured to formal charges.

JUDGE   To be charged is not to be convicted.

(The chains rattle.)

N'ZEKOU   I beg to differ, Your Honor. Six months detention with a dismissal, five months detention with an acquittal, seven months detention with a dismissal, three months detention at the end of which the penalty was fifteen days in prison sentence suspended, and, for the past two months, it's been prison again. I think I'd have done better being born in prison. Then they'd have to let me out, throw me out instead of always throwing me in.

(The chains rattle.)

JUDGE   (leafing through files) Raise your right hand. Do you swear to tell the truth, the whole truth, and nothing but the truth?

N'ZEKOU   (raising his right hand) I do.

JUDGE   State your case.

N'ZEKOU   Your Honor, I swear by Heaven and Earth —

JUDGE   If you don't mind, just state your case, and keep Heaven and Earth out of it. Justice has recourse to neither Heaven nor Earth. The chariot of Justice passes by leaving pure, clear traces. Justice would no longer be Justice unless it were Justice.

(The chains rattle.)

Now saying Justice is Justice means it's suspended between Heaven and Earth and sheltered from all profane hands, from all occult powers and beyond all terrestrial oscillations and all atmospheric disturbances.

(The chains rattle.)

N'ZEKOU   Your Honor, by all that's dear to me, —

JUDGE   Justice needs peace and quiet to develop into Justice. Justice doesn't strike except upon mature consideration and after extended excogitation; in consequence, it never misses the mark. Its aim is true because it takes its time judging in order to judge the better. That's why we call it Justice with a capital J. If, by chance, it does miss the mark, it nevertheless remains Justice. State your case.

(Prolonged rattling of the chains.)

(Raising his voice) Will you stop all those chains! Will you silence all those chains! When Justice passes by, all chains must bow down. Or else Justice would no longer be Justice.

USHER AND POLICEMAN   Silence in court! Silence in court!

JUDGE   Gag them, men. Gag them. And that's an order, an order from Justice, which prides itself on dignity and decorum.

(The Assemblage murmurs its approval.)

Yes, gentlemen, its dignity and decorum. That is the real, the true Justice. (To N'Zekou.) You are charged with impugning the honor of men of great substance, of upstanding and loyal citizens.

N'ZEKOU   Upstanding and loyal!

JUDGE   Yes, I choose my words wisely, "upstanding and loyal."

N'ZEKOU   Your Honor, I stipulate having said "Thôgô-gnini is a crook, a thief." I say it in front of you, in front of the Court because it's true. I proclaim it here and now. "Monsieur Thôgô-gnini is a thief."

JUDGE   Watch what you're saying. Monsieur Thôgô-gnini is a man of substance.

N'ZEKOU   For me, he is and always will be a thief, Your Honor.

JUDGE   Do you understand the situation?

N'ZEKOU   What situation?

JUDGE   That you've slanderously impugned the honor of an important man.

N'ZEKOU   Yes, I've called a thief a thief. I understand that much, Your Honor.

JUDGE   Well enough. But there's more. You're accused of being the leader of a gang known as "The Two Fingers."

N'ZEKOU   "The Two Fingers."

JUDGE   The gang that makes a clean sweep of markets and public squares.

N'ZEKOU   It's a lie, Your Honor.

JUDGE   I'm not finished; in fact, I've scarcely begun. You're also accused of being a member of the gang that kidnaps children and murders women on the highway from Pobou to Grabah.

N'ZEKOU   Your Honor, I'm reeling from the impact of these charges.

JUDGE   No, stand up. Before Justice, one stands steady, straight, and strong, albeit humble. Correct your posture; look Justice in the eye; it will reign supreme.

(The chains rattle.)

Call the first witness.

CLERK   Usher, summon Mademoiselle Ya-Gba.

USHER   Mademoiselle Ya-Gba. Madame Ya-Gba. Ya-Gba.

(Enter Ya-Gba.)

JUDGE   State your full name and occupation.

YA-GBA   Ya-Gba Couloughe, the Codjara district.

JUDGE   Your age?

YA-GBA   Huh?

JUDGE   Your age?

YA-GBA   My age?

JUDGE   Yes, your age?

YA-GBA   Fifteen, Your Honor.

(The Assemblage bursts out laughing.)

Are you suggesting I'm not fifteen? Take a good look.

(The Assemblage laughs again.)

Of course. I've miscalculated, Your Honor. I'm ten.

JUDGE   All right, I get the picture. But now, raise your right hand, and swear to tell the truth, the whole truth, and nothing but the truth.

YA-GBA   *(raising her right hand)* I swear by the heads of my six children.

JUDGE   Never mind the heads of your six children, just take the oath.

YA-GBA   *(quickly)* I swear by the heads of my mother, my father, my grandfather, my —

JUDGE   No. You don't swear by anyone's head in my court. Justice is anonymous; far above everyone, it has no ties with anyone. Therefore, you must swear quite simply to tell the truth, the whole truth and nothing but the truth.

YA-GBA   I do.

JUDGE   What have you to depose?

YA-GBA   One day, in front of the Café Lesoulard, the accused asked me to have a drink with him.

JUDGE   And?

YA-GBA   He wouldn't give any money to a beggar asking for alms.

JUDGE   And?

YA-GBA   (*racking her brain*) And . . . and . . . I met him one night when he was drunk. He grabbed me in his arms . . . and then . . . . (*She weeps and sobs.*) And then, Your Honor . . . and then . . . .

JUDGE   What happened next?

YA-GBA   What's that, Your Honor? What happened next? O my sainted Mother! What happened next? Your Honor? What happened next? My sainted mother!

JUDGE   Next witness.

CLERK   Summon the next witness, Monsieur Fakron.

USHER   Fakron! Fakron!

(*Enter Fakron.*)

FAKRON   Here! Here!

YA-GBA   What happened next, Your Honor? What happened next? (*Exit weeping.*)

FAKRON   Your Honor, may the sky fall on my head if I

don't tell the truth.

JUDGE   Not so fast.

FAKRON   May the ground slip from under my feet if I don't tell the truth. I've always told the truth. And I always, always shall tell it.

JUDGE   Will you raise your right hand and swear to tell the truth, the whole truth, and nothing but the truth?

FAKRON   Your Honor, I'm a Muslim. I swear by nothing, but the Koran, I know no other truth than the truth of the Koran. My God is the God of the Koran. What must I do?

(The chains rattle.)

JUDGE   *(slowly)* Tell the truth, the whole truth, and nothing but the truth. Raise your right hand, and say, "I do."

(Fakron raises his left hand.)

Your right hand.

FAKRON   I'm left-handed, Your Honor.

JUDGE   Not in the eyes of Justice. Justice is right-handed. Justice does nothing by heart and everything by reason, nothing with the left hand and everything with the right. Will you raise your right hand and swear to tell the truth, the whole truth, and nothing but the truth?

FAKRON   *(raising his left hand)* I do.

JUDGE   The right hand, I said!

FAKRON   Your Honor, for me, the left hand is the right hand.

JUDGE   True enough, but not in the Temple of Justice. Here, the right hand is the right hand and the left, the left. No compromises, no possibility of confusion. I therefore direct you to raise your right hand and swear to tell the truth, the whole truth, and nothing but the truth.

FAKRON   *(raising his right hand)* I swear to tell the truth, the whole truth, and nothing but the truth.

JUDGE   At last! Do you know this gentleman?

FAKRON   Yes, Your Honor. A few days ago, he stole ten million dollars from Monsieur Thôgô-gnini.

JUDGE   Exactly how many days ago?

FAKRON   *(with certainty)* A fortnight.

JUDGE   But the accused has been locked up for a good

two months.

FAKRON   Not true!

JUDGE   I beg your pardon.

FAKRON   Not true! Not true!

JUDGE   Not true? Not true?

FAKRON   What I mean is you don't know this man,
Your Honor. He's a rough customer and extremely
dangerous. He's a member of a gang that kidnaps and
murders on the highway.

(*Prolonged rattling of the chains.*)

JUDGE   Have you any proof to offer?

FAKRON   It's in the possession of Monsieur Thôgô-
gnini.

JUDGE   How do you know?

FAKRON   He told me so, himself.

JUDGE   When did he tell you?

FAKRON   This morning.

JUDGE   How much did he give you to say that?

76

FAKRON   Nothing as yet, but it will be forthcoming.

JUDGE   *(repeating Fakron's words)* "But it will be forthcoming."

(Prolonged rattling of the chains fills the courtroom.)

All those here present and anywhere else, whoever you may be, wherever you may be, I direct you to silence all chains while Justice is at work. *(To Fakron.)* In sum, what specific evidence do you have?

FAKRON   What I've told you: This man is dangerous and capable of . . . of . . . of . . . .

JUDGE   You may speak freely.

FAKRON   Of . . . of . . . I've completely forgotten, Your Honor.

JUDGE   Forgotten what?

FAKRON   Everything I'm supposed to say.

JUDGE   Oh, everything you're supposed to say.

FAKRON   Yes, Your Honor. In your presence, I came to know fear. Justice is so awesome. Your Honor . . . . If only you knew Monsieur Thôgô-gnini. Thôgô-gnini, oh, that Monsieur Thôgô-gnini. Thôgô-gnini, Your Honor . . . . Save us from Monsieur Thôgô-gnini,

Your Honor.

JUDGE   Have you anything more to depose?

FAKRON   Yes, Your Honor.

JUDGE   What?

(*Fakron suddenly becomes cautious and mistrustingly looks over the Judge, the Policemen, etc.*)

What?

FAKRON   Save us from Thôgô-gnini. I'm his friend. But that can't last. Everything's subject to change. Thôgô-gnini's changing into a scourge. Already, he's more dangerous than death what with his flattering some, lying to others, and defrauding everybody. Your Honor, tell the king what's going on. He would rule a happy people; he reigns over dead dreams . . . over ghosts . . . . Tell the king . . . .

JUDGE   The court takes note of your deposition. Next witness.

CLERK   Usher, summon the woman known as Brouba.

USHER   Madame Brouba! Brouba!

(*Enter Brouba.*)

JUDGE   Raise your right hand. Do you swear to tell the truth, the whole truth, and nothing but the truth?

BROUBA   I do.

JUDGE   What do you know of the crimes with which Monsieur N'Zekou is charged?

BROUBA   I'm his sister.

JUDGE   The Court rules that your evidence is admissible. You may testify.

BROUBA   Your Honor, I'm the guilty party.

JUDGE   What are you telling me?

BROUBA   My brother, N'Zekou, is innocent. I ought to be in his place; I'm ready to take his place.

JUDGE   Explain yourself more fully.

BROUBA   Your Honor, I'm the one who told my brother to go collect the sum Monsieur Thôgô-gnini owed him, because we had nothing in the house.

JUDGE   Come now, Madam, nothing in the house in this country?

BROUBA   Such a thing can happen, and it does happen that there's nothing in the house in even this country.

JUDGE   In your house, you mean.

BROUBA   In even the houses of others, Your Honor, in even the houses of others.

JUDGE   Go on.

BROUBA   My brother left. As he didn't return, I went to Monsieur Thôgô-gnini's. He subjected me to such treatment. Oh, Your Honor. That Monsieur Monsieur Thôgô-gnini, Your Honor!

JUDGE   You digress, Madam.

BROUBA   He called his servants who roughed me up. Oh, Your Honor, if you could have seen how they treated me.

JUDGE   All the same, Madam, this file on your brother and these witnesses.

BROUBA   He's done nothing beyond seeking what's owed him.

JUDGE   That's what you say. The charges against him are both serious and abundant. *(Reading.)* "Impugning the honor of a man of substance, leading a gang, theft."

BROUBA   No, Your Honor, none of this is possible.

JUDGE   *(reading)* "Theft, murder, kidnapping women

and children."

BROUBA   No! Your Honor, it isn't possible; it isn't true. You mustn't believe what these persons tell you. No, Your Honor, my brother is no thief, no murderer.

JUDGE   Madam!

BROUBA   I swear to you, Your Honor. My brother is no murderer, no thief. I stand ready to hold my hand in fire.

JUDGE   Whatever you do, don't do that.

BROUBA   My hand in fire, Your Honor, to prove I have faith in him and that I'm telling the truth.

JUDGE   Have you anything further to add?

BROUBA   Yes, Your Honor.

JUDGE   Good! What?

BROUBA   Dispense justice to my brother. I know he's innocent because Messieurs Kouame, Kablan, Ehoulé, Ahizi, Abou, Miezan, Kodjo, Brou, Tanoé, Kofit, and Abri were, like him, each in turn, victims of Monsieur Thôgô-gnini's dirty deals and, like him, arrested. Ah, justice, Your Honor, justice. We're so unhappy. (*She weeps.*) Unhappy. (*She weeps.*) Unhappy, Your Honor, unhappy.

JUDGE   (dreamily) Justice! Justice!

BROUBA   Yes, justice, Your Honor. I have faith in you. (Going.) We all have faith in you. (Exit.)

JUDGE   Next witness.

CLERK   Usher, summon the witness, Bouadi.

(Enter Bouadi.)

N'ZEKOU   You here? For what?

BOUADI   To testify.

JUDGE   Raise your right hand. Do you swear to tell the truth, the whole truth, and nothing but the truth?

BOUADI   (raising both hands) I —

JUDGE   No, only the right hand.

(Bouadi raises his right hand.)

That's it. Now say, "I do."

N'ZEKOU   Testify against me. You, too?

BOUADI   Why not? It's a paying job. Why not? Yes, even I have come to testify against you. These days, you have to forge ahead to keep your head above water . . .

keep your head above water. Your Honor, what do you want me to say?

JUDGE   What have you to say?

BOUADI   Anything you like. I'm prepared for anything.

JUDGE   He's a robber.

BOUADI   He's a robber.

JUDGE   He's a thief.

BOUADI   He's a thief.

JUDGE   He's a murderer.

BOUADI   He's a murderer.

JUDGE   "I'm a liar."

BOUADI   I'm a liar.

(The Judge laughs. Bouadi laughs.)

JUDGE   (shaking his head) What wicked times!

BOUADI   (shaking his head) What wicked times!

N'ZEKOU   (to Bouadi) You're not the man you were.

BOUADI Who is the man he was in this great whirligig, this free-for-all of a struggle for survival? Survival, my friend, survival. We're totally wretched creatures, pitiful creatures. *(He weeps.)* Survival! Ah, God protect us from the rage for survival! We're not ourselves any more. I've come to testify against you out of cowardice, out of fear of Monsieur Thôgô-gnini because he knows I'm your friend. Yes, out of cowardice.

N'ZEKOU How sad!

BOUADI Yes, yes. Forgive me. Oh, survival! Survival! Forgive me!

N'ZEKOU Yes. Go. Go survive. Survive!

JUDGE Next witness.

N'ZEKOU Still more witnesses?

CLERK Usher, summon the lady, Akaboua.

USHER Madame Akaboua. Akaboua.

(Enter Akaboua followed by two Young Men.)

N'ZEKOU My wife! My sons! Here to testify against me!

JUDGE State your name, occupation and marital status.

AKABOUA   Madame N'Zekou Paul, housewife, married, seven children, residing in Brotchikno.

JUDGE   Raise your right hand. Do you swear to tell the truth, the whole truth, and nothing but the truth?

AKABOUA   I do.

JUDGE   What have you to tell us?

AKABOUA   I've come . . . . *(She and her husband exchange glances.)* I've come . . . . *(She and the Judge exchange glances.)* Oh, Your Honor, if only you knew what's going on, if only you knew! Oh, survival! I've come . . . . No, I won't testify against my husband. I've come, Your Honor, to beg for his acquittal. I know he's committed no crime, that he's one of the victims of Monsieur Thôgô-gnini. There are scores of victims of Monsieur Thôgô-gnini. Your Honor, in our home, the hearth is cold, and joy is in exile. Poverty has taken its place. To us, you are Providence; on your judgement, will depend our happiness, our very lives, the happiness, the very lives of seven children, death or joy for countless households. Your Honor, you hold in your hands the fates of many families, the outcome of their dreams. It devolves upon you to bring them to life, to reintroduce them to life, to joy, to dancing. Your honor, the day is so beautiful when it's dawning, when it hesitantly wonders whether to revive, to return to mankind. It's so beautiful to hear a bird singing as it sits unconstrained on a branch or hops unrestrained through the grass; beautiful is the free laughter of men. With a gesture, a deed, a word, make, I beg of you, Your Honor, make daylight dawn. Daylight, Your Honor, daylight! *(Exit repeating her last word.)* Daylight, daylight!

JUDGE   This is my decision. You're a free man, Monsieur N'Zekou.

N'ZEKOU   Free! Free! Thank you, Your Honor! Free at last! Free at last!

JUDGE   *(rising and walking stage center)* Yes, free. Come what may, I mean to dispense true Justice. Here are my hands, my neck, my feet; shackle them with all the chains in the world . . . but, please liberate man from all chains.

(Noise and voices in the wings. A Crowd gesturing wildly, bursts into the courtroom, dragging with them Monsieur Thôgô-gnini dressed in his gunnysack suit.)

JUDGE   *(As if to himself)* Liberate man from all chains.

(Enter a Herald.)

HERALD   So it shall be, Your Honor. Our king has understood. In order to break all the chains, to bring joy back to life, to establish a haven of peace in our city, the chains must shackle Thôgô-gnini; he's the one to put on trial.

CROWD   Justice! Justice! (*They bring Thôgô-gnini before the Judge.*)

N'ZEKOU   Free at last! Free! Free!

(*The Crowd removes the chains from N'Zekou and puts them on Thôgô-gnini, at whom they jeer.*)

THÔGÔ-GNINI   But I'm Monsieur Thôgô-gnini!

CROWD   Justice! Justice! (*Jeering at Thôgô-gnini, the exuberant Crowd puts N'Zekou on their shoulders vociferously crying out.*) Free! Free! Free! (*Singing. Dancing.*)

CURTAIN

THE END

∽